THE
eat
light

Recipe Journal

Adapting Your Favorite Recipes for Healthful, Delicious Eating

Packed with fat- and calorie-saving cooking and baking swaps!

by Jessica Cohn
Concept by Claudine Gandolfi

PETER PAUPER PRESS, INC.
WHITE PLAINS, NEW YORK

To the staff at Peter Pauper Press

Designed by Margaret Rubiano

Copyright © 2011
Peter Pauper Press, Inc.
202 Mamaroneck Avenue
White Plains, NY 10601
All rights reserved
ISBN 978-1-4413-0527-5
Printed in Hong Kong
7 6 5 4 3 2 1

Visit us at www.peterpauper.com

CONTENTS

INTRODUCTION

We all collect recipes, whether we write them out on index cards, photocopy them from books and magazines, or print them out from the Internet. Our favorites—like grandma's lasagna or dad's secret BBQ sauce—pay homage to our loved ones. Others—like friends' and neighbors' soul-satisfying potluck crowd pleasers—keep us connected to community.

But you know it's true: Some of our most treasured dishes are way too rich for today's tastes and downright detrimental to one's health. Let's face it—comfort food fat and calories can be off the charts. The butter! The cheese! The sugar! The cream! (Not to mention the guilt!)

That's where *The Eat Light Recipe Journal* comes in. Within these pages you'll find multiple tips to help you improve the recipes that mean the most to you. Love beef Stroganoff but not the 400-plus calories and 26-plus grams of fat per serving? Simply swap in a few light ingredients (such as leaner beef, lower-fat, lower-sodium cream of mushroom soup, and fat-free sour cream) and—ta da! You've cut that dish down to (diet) size. You'll find space in this journal to record the new streamlined version you've adapted. Our lists of swap ideas will help get you going; resources and measuring charts provide handy references. So—bake that cake and eat it too! And write down the recipe for posterity.

The Eat Light Recipe Journal is a super tool in your quest to cut calories and fat, and add satisfaction! No one has to resort to dull packaged, processed diet meals or give up old favorites to get trimmer and healthier. Making small but significant swaps when cooking and baking will lower caloric and fat intake. And these small swaps may, over time, lead to big changes in your waistline, your energy level, and your life.

Look over the ingredients of any menu or recipe you're considering and think about possible swaps.

If, for instance, you're making vegetable dip for a family gathering, zero in on the amount of cream cheese needed. It's not news that cream cheese is caloric and high in fat. So try lower-cal and/or lower-fat alternatives that offer a similar taste.

Sample cream cheese swaps:

Instead of **cream cheese** (1 oz), 97 calories, 9.71 grams fat

- **Neufchâtel** (1 oz), 72 calories, 6.46 grams fat
  You save 25 calories, 3.25 grams fat.

- **Ricotta cheese, part skim** (1 oz), 39 calories, 2.24 grams fat
  You save 58 calories, 7.47 grams fat.

- **Cream cheese, fat-free** (1 oz), 27 calories, .39 grams fat
  You save 70 calories, 9.32 grams fat.

- **Cottage cheese, 1% milk fat** (1 oz), 20.25 calories, .30 grams fat
  You save 76.75 calories, 9.41 grams fat.

- **Greek yogurt, fat-free** (1 oz), 15 calories, 0 grams fat
  You save 82 calories, 9.71 grams fat.

FOOD FOR THOUGHT

Make the most of your meals!

- Use fresh ingredients. Cook in bulk and freeze extra servings.

- Buy leaner cuts of meat and fresh, locally produced fruits and vegetables. Include more whole grains in your meal planning. Being choosy makes a difference!

- Reduce your use of condiments, gravies, and sauces. One cup of canned turkey gravy is 121 calories. Maybe a spoonful will do!

- Avoid heart-*unhealthy* saturated fats and dietary cholesterol (sources: animal products, such as meat, poultry, and dairy; lard and butter; and tropical, coconut, and palm oils) and trans fats (partially hydrogenated vegetable oils; french fries; commercial baked goods such as cookies and doughnuts; and shortening and margarine). Instead, swap in monounsaturated and polyunsaturated fats and omega-3 fatty acids. Snack on sunflower or pumpkin seeds. Use canola oil, olive oil, flaxseed oil, and walnut oil. Other sources: all-natural peanut butter, avocados, salmon, and mackerel.

- About half your daily calories should come from carbohydrates, which consist of sugars, starches, and fiber. So if you're eating 1,500 calories per day, 750 of them (188 grams) should be from carbs. Strive to get those calories from fresh fruits and veggies and whole grains. Avoid bleached flour, refined sugar, and high fructose corn syrup.

- Enhance your food with flavor. Sprinkle dishes with fresh herbs just before serving. Try a marinade (an oil, an acid, and aromatics: spices and herbs) to add pizzazz to lean cuts of meat. Dry rubs (herbs, spices, and other seasonings) can bring out the best in meats, too.

- Use texture. Top your burger with a slice of creamy, heart-healthy avocado instead of cheese. Or add diced avocado to salads.

Swap in a cup of old-fashioned oatmeal for a cup of flour to add yummy texture to your next batch of chocolate chip cookies. Or try adding oatmeal to that turkey "meatloaf."

- How you cook is as important as what you cook. Every table-spoon of oil used for frying adds 14 grams of fat and over 100 calories. Consider methods that require little or no oil, such as poaching and steaming, and methods that allow the fat within food to drip away as it cooks, such as grilling and broiling.

- New research from the Harvard School of Public Health associates consumption of processed meats, such as deli meats, hot dogs, and bacon, with a higher risk of heart disease and type 2 diabetes. The study did not find higher risks among those eating unprocessed meat. So ... watch your intake of smoked, cured, or salted meats, or those with added chemical preservatives.

- Cut the salt and watch the sodium content of foods you eat. Excess sodium causes water retention (and subsequent weight gain) as well as a host of health problems. Folks who keep sodium levels low report faster weight loss, lower blood pressure, and more energy. The USDA now recommends you consume no more than 1500 grams of sodium per day. So read the labels and compare sodium content—you may be surprised at how much sodium is in your favorite fast food meal or bowl of cereal. When cooking, instead of salt, boost flavor with onion, garlic, or with a splash of lemon juice, wine, or balsamic vinegar. And don't forget the herbs and spices. In one study, overweight people who sprinkled their food with zero-calorie spices lost an average of 30 pounds in six months.

Your smart choices will add up!

Supermarket shelves overwhelm us with chips, crackers, and "goodies" of all sorts. Popular restaurants lure us with cheese-smothered appetizers and "death by" desserts. What's a mere mortal to do?

Put those cravings in two capable hands—your own! When you hanker for higher cal, unhealthy foods, try thinking of other ways to get the same sweet taste or salty crunch. And then make those choices a habit. In this section, you'll find simple swaps to help you get started, organized in three sections:

Second-Thought Swaps. Easy ideas to help you shop for pantry items and order when you're eating out:

On second thought, a bowl of steel-cut or old-fashioned oatmeal with cinnamon and a few apple slices would make a much more satisfying alternative to that greasy, high-cal, high-fat, fast-food muffin.

Swaps for Cooking and Baking. Good substitutes for homemade creations.

Make your own breakfast muffins, subbing mashed banana or applesauce for shortening and cutting down on the eggs. Freeze some for smarter quick starts on busy mornings.

Healthful Swaps. Ways to boost nutrition and fiber—and end up feeling happier about everything you cook and eat!

According to the American Grassfed Association (americangrassfed.org), grassfed animal products are lower in fat, cholesterol, and calories, and higher in omega-3 fatty acids, among other health benefits, than grain-fed counterparts. (Keep in mind that these meats are also known for their distinctive "grassy" flavor and cooking qualities, too.)

Ready to change your life? Let this **Eat Light Recipe Journal** help you focus on your goals!

Use the swaps that follow and get started. Just keep your eyes on the prize (losing weight, feeling better) instead of the fries!

By the way, instead of frying those fries, cut and bake potato strips (including the skin!) sprinkled with herbs. Smart swap—potatoes are an excellent source of potassium.

There are two ways these swaps work:

- They'll help you substitute lower-cal, lower-fat ingredients in your recipes.
- They'll make you more mindful of prepared foods that you eat and serve, such as breads, cereals, and snacks.

The more you cook and bake yourself, the more you control your fat and calorie intake. And the more you stock your fridge, freezer, and cupboards with grocery swap-ins, the faster you'll see and feel the results.

Two questions to ask when selecting prepared items:

- Is there a healthier, lower-cal version?
- Would something less fattening be just as satisfying?

For example, when you have a "taste" for burgers, stop and think. Is it the meat you crave? The bun? The special sauce? Sub in leaner meat. Or heartier whole wheat bread. Or zesty, nearly zero-calorie horseradish. Paying attention to your hankerings can pay off.

Notes: As much as possible, the calorie and fat information provided is based on the USDA Nutrient Database (http://www.nal.usda.gov/fnic/foodcomp/search/) and on product labels, but fat and calories vary by source and brand. Also, we've tried to include swaps of benefit for everyone, but some are higher in sodium than we'd like. Sodium watchers, check those labels!

SECOND-THOUGHT SWAPS

Instead of	Swap	You save!
Bagel, medium plain (1 bagel), 289 calories, 1.68 grams fat	**Lender's 100 Calorie Bagel**, plain, (1 bagel), 100 calories, 1 gram fat	**189** calories, **.68** grams fat
Barbecue sauce (2 tbsp), 52 calories, 0 grams fat	**Salsa** (2 tbsp), 9 calories, 0 grams fat	**43** calories, **0** grams fat
Beef jerky (1 oz), 115 calories, 7.26 grams fat	**Turkey jerky** (1 oz), 80 calories, 1 gram fat	**35** calories, **6.26** grams fat
Biscuit, refrigerated dough, lower fat (2-¼"), 63 calories, 1.09 grams fat	**Breadstick** (1 plain), 7-⅝" x ⅝", 41 calories, .95 gram fat	**22** calories, **.14** grams fat
Bologna, pork, chicken, and beef (1 slice), 76 calories, 6.36 grams fat	**Turkey bologna** (1 serving), 59 calories, 4.49 grams fat	**17** calories, **1.87** grams fat
Bread, sandwich, white (for chicken or tuna salad), (2 slices), 132 calories, 2 grams fat	**Lettuce leaf** (1 large outer), 2 calories, .02 grams fat	**130** calories, **1.98** grams fat
Bread, sandwich, white, (2 slices), 132 calories, 2 grams fat	**Weight Watchers® 100% Whole Wheat Bread** (2 slices), 90 calories, 1 gram fat	**42** calories, **1** gram fat
Broccoli, frozen with cheese-flavored sauce, (1 cup), 113 calories, 4.20 grams fat	**Broccoli**, plain, cooked, (1 cup), 54 calories, .32 grams fat	**59** calories, **3.88** grams fat
Brownie, commercial (2-¾" square), 227 calories, 9 grams fat	**Light chocolate syrup** (2 tbsp) **on medium banana**, 155 calories, 0 grams fat	**72** calories, **9** grams fat
Bun, hamburger (1), 120 calories, 2 grams fat	**Arnold Sandwich Thins** (1 roll), 100 calories, 1 gram fat	**20** calories, **1** gram fat
Burger (fast food single with everything), 470 calories, 21 grams fat	**Child's burger** (single), 230 calories, 8 grams fat	**240** calories, **13** grams fat

Instead of	Swap	You save!
Butter for spread (1 tbsp), 102 calories, 11.52 grams fat	**Low-fat cream cheese** (1 tbsp), 30 calories, 2.29 grams fat	**72** calories, **9.23** grams fat
Butter for spread (1 tbsp), 102 calories, 11.52 grams fat	**Margarine spread with yogurt** (1 tbsp), 46 calories, 4.90 grams fat	**56** calories, **6.62** grams fat
Butter as topping (as on popcorn) (1 tbsp), 102 calories, 11.52 grams fat	**Parmesan cheese** (1 tbsp), 22 calories, 1.43 grams fat	**80** calories, **10.09** grams fat
Butter as topping (as on popcorn) (1 tbsp), 102 calories, 11.52 grams fat	**2 seconds of spray butter**, 14 calories, less than 2 grams fat (estimate)	**88** calories, at least **9.52** grams fat
Cake, pound, with butter (½ of 12-oz cake), 109 calories, 6 grams fat	**Angel food cake** (½ of 12-oz cake), 72 calories, 0 grams fat	**37** calories, **6** grams fat
Candy bar, plain milk chocolate, 210 calories, 13 grams fat	**Chocolate fat-free pudding cup**, 102 calories, 0 grams fat	**108** calories, **13** grams fat
Cereal, granola (1 cup), 412 calories, 12.35 grams fat	**Shredded wheat bites cereal** (1 cup), 167 calories, 1 gram fat	**245** calories, **11.35** grams fat
Cheese, American, pasteurized, processed (1 slice), 79 calories, 7 grams fat	**Cheese, American,** pasteurized, processed, low fat (1 slice), 38 calories, 1 gram fat	**41** calories, **6** grams fat
Chicken (fried, battered drumstick), 193 calories, 11.34 grams fat	**Chicken** (fried, battered drumstick, skin & bone removed), 82 calories, 3.39 grams fat	**111** calories, **7.95** grams fat
Coffee creamer, liquid, unflavored (1 tbsp), 20 calories, 1 gram fat	**Coffee creamer,** fat free, liquid, unflavored, (1 tbsp), 10 calories, 0 grams fat	**10** calories, **1** gram fat
Cookies, Oreo (2), 160 calories, 7 grams fat	**Oreo Fun Stix** (2), 90 calories, 3.5 grams fat	**70** calories, **3.50** grams fat
Crackers, wheat (16), 140 calories, 5 grams fat	**Matzo** (1), 111 calories, 0 grams fat	**29** calories, **5** grams fat

Instead of	Swap	You save!
Dunkin' Donuts Cinnamon Cake Donut (1), 340 calories, 22 grams fat	Nabisco Honey Maid Low-Fat Cinnamon Graham Crackers (1 serving), 140 calories, 2 grams fat	200 calories, 20 grams fat
English muffin, plain (1 muffin), 134 calories, 1.03 grams fat	Weight Watchers® low-fat English muffin, plain (1 muffin), 100 calories, 0 grams fat	34 calories, 1.03 grams fat
Fish stick (1 stick, frozen, breaded), 70 calories, 3.71 grams fat	Shrimp (4 large, cooked, moist heat), 22 calories, .24 grams fat	48 calories, 3.47 grams fat
French fries, baked from frozen (10 strips), 202 calories, 5 grams fat	Sweet potato, baked, no butter (1 medium), 103 calories, .17 grams fat	99 calories, 4.83 grams fat
French toast sticks (5), 371 calories, 19.34 grams fat	Multi-grain waffles (2), 142 calories, 2.24 grams fat	229 calories, 17.1 grams fat
Good Humor Strawberry Shortcake bar, 230 calories, 12 grams fat	Frozen strawberries, thawed (½ cup) & fat-free strawberry yogurt (½ cup), 91.83 calories, .12 grams fat	138.17 calories, 11.88 grams fat
Ham (1 slice), 46 calories, 2.41 grams fat	Extra-lean ham (1 slice), 29 calories, .70 grams fat	17 calories, 1.71 grams fat
Ham, regular (1 slice), 46 calories, 2.41 grams fat	Turkey ham (1 serving), 32 calories, 1.15 grams fat	14 calories, 1.26 grams fat
Hamburger with veggies & condiments, 512 calories, 27.36 grams fat	Mayo Clinic portobello mushroom "burger" with veggies & condiments, 283 calories, 9 grams fat	229 calories, 18.36 grams fat
Hormel Pepperoni (14 slices), 140 calories, 13 grams fat	Hormel Turkey Pepperoni (17 slices), 70 calories, 4 grams fat	70 calories, 9 grams fat
Hot dog, pork, 204 calories, 18 grams fat	Applegate Organic hot dog, turkey, 60 calories, 3.5 grams fat	144 calories, 14.50 grams fat
Ice cream, chocolate, "rich" (½ cup), 188.5 calories, 12.57 grams fat	Chocolate sorbet (½ cup), 130 calories, .50 grams fat	58.5 calories, 12.07 grams fat

Instead of	Swap	You save!
Ice cream, strawberry (½ cup), 127 calories, 5.54 grams fat	Breyer's Light Strawberry Yogurt Fat Free (½ cup), 53.33 calories, 0 grams fat	73.67 calories, 5.54 grams fat
Ice cream, vanilla, "rich" (½ cup), 266 calories, 17.33 grams fat	Frozen soft-serve vanilla yogurt (½ cup), 114 calories, 4.03 grams fat	152 calories, 13.30 grams fat
Ice cream, vanilla, "rich" (½ cup), 266 calories, 17.33 grams fat	Ice cream, light vanilla, no sugar added (½ cup), 105 calories, 5 grams fat	161 calories, 12.33 grams fat
Juice, orange-strawberry-banana (1 cup), 117 calories, .37 grams fat	Tomato juice (1 cup), 41 calories, .12 grams fat	76 calories, .25 grams fat
Kellogg's Cracklin' Oat Bran Cereal (¾ cup), 197 calories, 7 grams fat	Fiber One Cereal (¾ cup), 90 calories, 1 gram fat	107 calories, 6 grams fat
Lemonade (8 fluid oz), 110 calories, 0 grams fat	Water (8 fluid oz) with lemon juice (1 fluid oz), 8 calories, 0 grams fat	102 calories, 0 grams fat
Lemonade, from frozen concentrate (1 cup), 99 calories, .10 grams fat	Water & lemon (1 cup), 1 calorie, 0 grams fat	98 calories, 0.10 grams fat
Hellmann's Real Mayonnaise (1 tbsp), 90 calories, 10 grams fat	Hellmann's Light Mayonnaise (1 tbsp), 35 calories, 3.5 grams fat	55 calories, 6.5 grams fat
Hellmann's Real Mayonnaise (1 tbsp), 90 calories, 10 grams fat	Smart Balance Omega Plus Light Mayonnaise Dressing (1 tbsp), 50 calories, 4.5 grams fat	40 calories, 5.5 grams fat
Hellmann's Real Mayonnaise (1 tbsp), 90 calories, 10 grams fat	Mashed avocado (1 tbsp), 23 calories, 2.11 grams fat	67 calories, 7.89 grams fat
Macaroni & cheese, boxed, with milk & margarine (1 cup), 400 calories, 16.6 grams fat	Cauliflower & cheese, frozen, boxed (1 cup), 100 calories, 5 grams fat	300 calories, 11.6 grams fat
Margarita, from pre-made mix (5 oz), 312.5 calories, 0 grams fat	Red wine (5 oz), 125 calories, 0 grams fat	187.5 calories, 0 grams fat

Instead of	Swap	You save!
Martin's Sour Cream Onion Dip (2 tbsp), 60 calories, 5 grams fat	Salsa (2 tbsp), 9 calories, 0 grams fat	51 calories, 5 grams fat
Martin's Sour Cream Onion Dip (2 tbsp), 60 calories, 5 grams fat	Trader Joe's Fat-Free Spicy Black Bean Dip (2 tbsp), 30 calories, 0 grams fat	30 calories, 5 grams fat
Meatballs (4), 170 calories, 12 grams fat	Yves Classic Meatless Veggie Meatballs (4), 80 calories, 2 grams fat	90 calories, 10 grams fat
Milkshake, chocolate (8 oz), 272 calories, 6.16 grams fat	Chocolate milk, low fat (8 oz), 157.52 calories, 2.48 grams fat	114.48 calories, 3.68 grams fat
Muffin, blueberry, commercially prepared (1 medium), 444 calories, 21.74 grams fat	Muffin, homemade, low cal, low fat, (1 medium), 75 calories, .50 grams fat	369 calories, 21.24 grams fat
Muffin, blueberry, commercially prepared (1 medium), 444 calories, 21.74 grams fat	Quaker Old-Fashioned Oats (cooked, 1 serving), & apple (medium, ½ sliced) 197.50 calories, 3.16 grams fat	246.50 calories, 18.58 grams fat
Nuts, mixed, oil-roasted (1 cup), 876 calories, 79.99 grams fat	Chickpeas, canned (1 cup), 286 calories, 2.74 grams fat	590 calories, 77.25 grams fat
Pizza, slice of 14-inch pizza chain cheese pie, regular crust, 272 calories, 9.8 grams fat	Red bell pepper bruschetta, home recipe, (1 slice), 105 calories, 6.9 grams fat	167 calories, 2.9 grams fat
Popcorn, microwave buttered (⅔ cup), 150 calories, 9 grams fat	Plain air-popped popcorn (⅔ cup), 110 calories, 1 gram fat	40 calories, 8 grams fat
Potato chips (8-oz bag), 1217 calories, 82.63 grams fat	Popcorn snack, air-popped (8 oz), 880 calories, 10.32 grams fat	337 calories, 72.31 grams fat
Potatoes, mashed with whole milk and butter (1 cup), 237 calories, 8.86 grams fat	Sweet potato, baked, no butter (1 cup), 180 calories, .30 grams fat	57 calories, 8.56 grams fat
Pudding, vanilla instant with whole milk (1 cup), 324 calories, 8.24 grams fat	Pudding, vanilla, fat-free instant (1 cup), 60 calories, 0 grams fat	264 calories, 8.24 grams fat

Instead of	Swap	You save!
Roll/bun, hamburger or hot dog, plain (1) 120 calories, 1.86 grams fat	Roll/bun, hamburger or hot dog, reduced calorie (1), 84 calories, .86 grams fat	36 calories, 1 gram fat
Roll, sub, Italian (6"), 200 calories, 2 grams fat	Pita (4" diameter), 74 calories, .73 grams fat	126 calories, 1.27 grams fat
Salad dressing, balsamic vinaigrette with olive oil (1 tbsp), 45 calories, 4 grams fat	Lemon juice (1 tbsp), 3 calories, 0 grams fat	42 calories, 4 grams fat
Salad dressing, Caesar (1 tbsp), 80 calories, 8.5 grams fat	Balsamic vinegar (1 tbsp), 14 calories, 0 grams fat	66 calories, 8.5 grams fat
Salad dressing, Italian (1 tbsp), 43 calories, 4 grams fat	Salad dressing, Italian, fat-free (1 tbsp), 7 calories, 0 grams fat	36 calories, 4 grams fat
Salad dressing, ranch (1 tbsp), 73 calories, 7.71 grams fat	Bolthouse Farms Ranch Yogurt Dressing (1 tbsp), 35 calories, 3 grams fat	38 calories, 4.71 grams fat
Salad dressing, thousand island (1 tbsp), 59 calories, 5.61 grams fat	McDonald's Newman's Own Low Fat Balsamic Vinaigrette (1 tbsp), 10 calories, .69 grams fat	49 calories, 4.92 grams fat
Sheer Bliss Freedom Ice Cream with pomegranate & blueberry swirls (½ cup), 290 calories, 16 grams fat	Blueberries, frozen (½ cup), 84 calories, .49 grams fat	206 calories, 15.51 grams fat
Sour cream (1 cup), 444 calories, 45.38 grams fat	Fat-free Greek yogurt (1 cup), 120 calories, 0 grams fat	324 calories, 45.38 grams fat
Sour cream (1 cup), 444 calories, 45.38 grams fat	Fat-free sour cream (1 cup), 232 calories, 0 grams fat	212 calories, 45.38 grams fat
Sugar (1 tsp), 16 calories, 0 grams fat	Stevia clear liquid (2 drops), 0 calories, 0 grams fat	16 calories, 0 grams fat
Taco shell (5-in diameter), 150 calories, 6 grams fat	Flour tortilla (6 in), 90 calories, 1 gram fat	60 calories, 5 grams fat

Instead of	Swap	You save!
Tea, ready-to-drink sweetened (1 cup), 88 calories, 0 grams fat	**Plain tea** (1 cup), 2 calories, 0 grams fat	**86** calories, **0** grams fat
Tortilla chips, yellow corn, (8 oz), 1120 calories, 48 grams fat	**Sliced jicama** (1 cup), **lime juice** (1 oz), **chili powder** (½ tsp), 61 calories, .36 grams fat	**1059** calories, **47.64** grams fat
Tortilla chips, nacho cheese (1 oz), 146 calories, 7 grams fat	**Tortilla chips**, baked low-fat (1 oz), 118 calories, 2 grams fat	**28** calories, **5** grams fat
Wine, white (5 oz), 121 calories, 0 grams fat	**Spritzer**, wine (3 oz) & club soda (2 oz), 72 calories, 0 grams fat	**49** calories, **0** grams fat
Yogurt, plain (1 cup), 149 calories, 7.96 grams fat	**Yogurt, fat-free, plain** (1 cup), 137 calories, .44 grams fat	**12** calories, **7.52** grams fat

I feel a recipe is only a theme,
which an intelligent cook can play
each time with a variation.

MADAME BENOIT

SWAPS FOR COOKING AND BAKING

Ready for new adventures in the kitchen? The swaps that follow can lead you to delicious culinary discoveries.

The numbers provided are, as much as possible, based on the USDA Nutrient Database (http://www.nal.usda.gov/fnic/foodcomp/search/) or product labeling, though you should be aware of the following:

Calories and fat for the same food item differ by source or brand and by preparation method. The amount of fat and number of calories vary each time you prepare a recipe. So ... your tallies will always be approximations. More math: Some swaps are by the cup, others by the ounce or tablespoon. You'll find a handy guide to measures on pages 228–229. Keep in mind, too, that if one cup of milk is used in a recipe that yields eight servings, you'll of course divide fat and calorie values by eight to find single-serving amounts.

The fat and calorie listings here are offered as representative ratios of what you may save. And the list suggests general categories of swaps and does not attempt to provide them all.

A note about reduced-fat baking: The results will be different from traditional, higher-fat baking. Butter and other fats whip flavor and air into batter when combined with sugar, giving baked goods their texture. Fruit purées, especially unsweetened applesauce, help retain moisture. But the texture may differ. Try swapping out a little at a time and research others' baking tips online.

The point is to discover some of the tried-and-true ways smart cooks cut fat and calories while getting creative! Not every swap may work out perfectly the first time you try it. But as Julia Child once said, "No matter what happens in the kitchen, never apologize." Your time in the kitchen should be adventuresome and fun.

Instead of	Swap	You save!
Bacon, Oscar Mayer Hearty Thick Cut (1 serving), 60 calories, 5 grams fat	Bacon, Oscar Mayer Center Cut (1 serving), 50 calories, 4 grams fat	10 calories, 1 gram fat
Bacon, Oscar Mayer Hearty Thick Cut (1 serving), 60 calories, 5 grams fat	Turkey Bacon, Butterball Thin & Crispy (1 serving) 30 calories, 2 grams fat	30 calories, 3 grams fat
Beef, ground, 30% fat, raw (1 oz), 93 calories, 8 grams fat	Beef, ground, grassfed, raw (1 oz), 54 calories, 4 grams fat	39 calories, 4 grams fat
Beef, ground, 30% fat, patty, broiled (3 oz), 232 calories, 15 grams fat	Ground turkey, patty, cooked (3 oz), 145 calories, 7.56 grams fat	87 calories, 7.44 grams fat
Beef, ground, 30% fat, patty, broiled (3 oz), 232 calories, 15 grams fat	Beef, ground, 5% fat, patty, pan-browned (3 oz), 139 calories, 5 grams fat	93 calories, 10 grams fat
Beef, ground, 30% fat, patty, broiled (3 oz), 232 calories, 15 grams fat	MorningStar Farms Meal Starters Grillers Recipe Crumbles, meatless (⅔ cup), 80 calories, 2.5 grams fat	152 calories, 12.5 grams fat
Biscuit, refrigerated dough (large), 193 calories, 8.41 grams fat	Biscuit, refrigerated dough, lower fat (2-¼"), 63 calories, 1.09 grams fat	130 calories, 7.32 grams fat
Bread crumbs, seasoned (1 cup), 460 calories, 6.58 grams fat	Japanese Panko bread crumbs (1 cup), 220 calories, 1 gram fat	240 calories, 5.58 grams fat
Bread crumbs, seasoned (1 cup), 460 calories, 6.58 grams fat	Oatmeal, old-fashioned, (1 cup) 300 calories, 6 grams fat	160 calories, .58 grams fat
Broth, chicken, canned (1 cup), 40 calories, 2 grams fat	Broth, chicken, 99% fat-free (1 cup), 10 calories, .50 grams fat	30 calories, 1.5 grams fat
Butter, as flavoring (1 tbsp), 102 calories, 11.52 grams fat	Broth, chicken, fat-free (4 tbsp), 1.25 calories, 0 grams fat	100.75 calories, 11.52 grams fat
Butter, as flavoring (1 tbsp), 102 calories, 11.52 grams fat	Broth, roasted garlic & chicken, fat-free (4 tbsp), 5.25 calories, .01 grams fat	96.75 calories, 11.51 grams fat

Instead of	Swap	You save!
Butter, for baking (1 cup), 1628 calories, 184.12 grams fat	**Butter** (½ cup) **& natural peanut butter** (½ cup), 1574 calories, 156.06 grams fat	**54** calories, **28.06** grams fat
Butter, for baking (1 cup), 1628 calories, 184.12 grams fat	**Butter** (½ cup) **& unsweetened applesauce** (½ cup), 865 calories, 104.06 grams fat	**763** calories, **80.06** grams fat
Butter, for baking (1 cup), 1628 calories, 184.12 grams fat	**Butter** (½ cup) **& ricotta cheese, part-sklm** (½ cup), 983.50 calories, 101.73 grams fat	**644.50** calories, **82.39** grams fat
Butter, for baking (1 cup), 1628 calories, 184.12 grams fat	**Butter** (½ cup) **& bananas, mashed** (½ cup), 914 calories, 92.43 grams fat	**714** calories, **91.69** grams fat
Butter, for frying (1 tbsp), 102 calories, 11.52 grams fat	**4 seconds olive oil spray**, 28 calories, less than 4 grams fat	**74** calories, & over **7.52** grams fat
Butter, for sautéing (1 tbsp), 102 calories, 11.52 grams fat	**Cooking wine** (4 tbsp), 28 calories, 0 grams fat	**74** calories, **11.52** grams fat
Butter, for sautéing (1 tbsp), 102 calories, 11.52 grams fat	**Flat beer** (3 tbsp), 20 calories, 0 grams fat	**82** calories, **11.52** grams fat
Butter, for sautéing (1 tbsp), 102 calories, 11.52 grams fat	**Veggie broth** (4 tbsp), 3 calories, 0 grams fat	**99** calories, **11.52** grams fat
Butter, for sautéing (1 tbsp), 102 calories, 11.52 grams fat	**Margarine-like light spread** (1 tbsp), 47 calories, 5.1 grams fat	**55** calories, **6.42** grams fat
Cheese, cheddar, shredded (1 cup), 479 calories, 36.3 grams fat	**Cheese, cheddar, low-fat,** shredded (1 cup), 195 calories, 7.91 grams fat	**284** calories, **28.39** grams fat
Cheese, mozzarella, whole milk (1 cup), 336 calories, 25.03 grams fat	**Cheese, cottage, 1% milk** fat (1 cup), 163 calories, 2.31 grams fat	**173** calories, **22.72** grams fat
Cheese, mozzarella, whole milk (1 cup), 336 calories, 25.03 grams fat	**Cheese, mozzarella, nonfat, shredded** (1 cup), 159 calories, 0 grams fat	**177** calories, **25.03** grams fat

Instead of	Swap	You save!
Cheese sauce, prepared, from recipe (1 cup), 479 calories, 36.26 grams fat	Cheese sauce (½ cup), & butternut squash purée (½ cup), 321.50 calories, 18.31 grams fat	**157.5** calories, **17.95** grams fat
Chicken breast (½ breast), fried, battered, boneless, 364 calories, 18.48 grams fat	Chicken breast (½ breast), roasted, skinless, boneless, 142 calories, 3.07 grams fat	**222** calories, **15.41** grams fat
Chili con carne, with beans (1 cup), 298 calories, 12.94 grams fat	Chili, Hormel Vegetarian, with beans (1 cup), 190 calories, 1 gram fat	**108** calories, **11.94** grams fat
Corn syrup (¼ cup), 240 calories, 0 grams fat	Brown rice syrup (¼ cup), 168 calories, 0 grams fat	**72** calories, **0** grams fat
Cream, for cooking, table cream (1 cup), 468 calories, 46.34 grams fat	Evaporated skim milk (1 cup), 200 calories, .51 grams fat	**268** calories, **45.83** grams fat
Cream, for gravy or sauce (1 cup), 315 calories, 27.83 grams fat	Evaporated skim milk (1 cup), 200 calories, .51 grams fat	**115** calories, **27.32** grams fat
Cream, for soup, table cream (1 cup), 468 calories, 46.34 grams fat	Fage Total 0% Greek yogurt (1 cup), 120 calories, 0 grams fat	**348** calories, **46.34** grams fat
Cream, for soup, table cream (1 cup), 468 calories, 46.34 grams fat	Silken soft tofu (2 slices), 170 calories, 8 grams fat	**298** calories, **38.34** grams fat
Cream, for thickening, table cream (1 cup), 468 calories, 46.34 grams fat	Nonfat milk (1 cup), & Argo cornstarch (2 tbsp), 143 calories, .20 grams fat	**325** calories, **46.14** grams fat
Cream, for thickening, table cream (1 oz), 39 calories, 3.47 grams fat	Instant mashed potatoes (1 tbsp), 11 calories, 0 grams fat	**28** calories, **3.47** grams fat
Cream, heavy whipping for topping (5 oz), 515 calories, 55.15 grams fat	Whipped canned evaporated nonfat milk (5 oz) & lemon (1 tsp), 126 calories, 0.31 grams fat	**389** calories, **54.84** grams fat
Cream, fluid, heavy, whipped (2 tbsp), 51.75 calories, 5.55 gram fat	Whipped Reddi-wip fat-free whipped cream (2 tbsp), 5 calories, 0 grams fat	**46.75** calories, **5.55** grams fat

Instead of	Swap	You save!
Egg (1 large), 72 calories, 4.75 grams fat	**Egg substitute, liquid fat-free** (4 tbsp), 29 calories, 0 grams fat	**43** calories, **4.75** grams fat
Egg (1 large), 72 calories, 4.75 grams fat	**Egg whites** (2 large), 34 calories, .12 grams fat	**38** calories, **4.63** grams fat
Flour, all-purpose, for thickening stew (½ cup), 227.5 calories, .62 grams fat	**Grated potato** (1 small), 131 calories, .15 grams fat	**96.5** calories, **.47** grams fat
Hamburger meat 70% lean (3 oz), 230 calories, 15.18 grams fat	**Ground turkey,** 93% lean broiled patty (3 oz), 176 calories, 9.73 grams fat	**54** calories, **5.45** grams fat
Heavy cream unwhipped (1 cup), 821 calories, 88.06 grams fat	**Evaporated skim milk** (1 cup), 200 calories, .51 grams fat	**621** calories, **87.55** grams fat
Heavy cream, fluid, whipped (1 cup), 414 calories, 44.40 grams fat	**Frozen dessert topping** (1 cup), 238 calories, 18.98 grams fat	**176** calories, **25.42** grams fat
Heavy cream, fluid, whipped (1 cup), 414 calories, 44.40 grams fat	**Light cream,** fluid, whipped (1 cup), 350 calories, 37.09 grams fat	**64** calories, **7.31** grams fat
Hot dog, beef & pork (1), 137 calories, 12.44 grams fat	**Yves Meatless veggie dog** (1), 50 calories, .50 grams fat	**87** calories, **11.94** grams fat
Ketchup (2 tbsp), 30 calories, .10 grams fat	**Tomato,** large (thick slice), 5 calories, .05 grams fat	**25** calories, **.05** grams fat
Milk, whole (1 cup), 146 calories, 8 grams fat	**Almond Breeze almond milk** (1 cup), 60 calories, 2.5 grams fat	**86** calories, **5.5** grams fat
Milk, whole (1 cup), 146 calories, 8 grams fat	**Milk, fat-free** (1 cup), 86 calories, 0 grams fat	**60** calories, **8** grams fat
Noodles, egg (1 cup), 221 calories, 3.31 grams fat	**Kelp noodles** (1 cup), 12 calories, 0 grams fat	**209** calories, **3.31** grams fat

Instead of	Swap	You save!
Noodles, egg (1 cup), 221 calories, 3.31 grams fat	Shirataki noodles (1 cup), 40 calories, 1 gram fat	181 calories, 2.31 grams fat
Nuts, for topping, chopped walnuts (1 cup), 765 calories, 76.30 grams fat	Oatmeal, rolled oats, (1 cup), 300 calories, 6 grams fat	465 calories, 70.3 grams fat
Pineapple slices, in heavy syrup (2 slices), 90 calories, 0 grams fat	Pineapple slices, in pineapple juice (2 slices), 60 calories, 0 grams fat	30 calories, 0 grams fat
Oil for baking, canola (1 cup), 1927 calories, 218 grams fat	Canola oil (½ cup) & purée of plums (½ cup), 1363.50 calories, 109 grams fat	563.50 calories, 109 grams fat
Oil for baking, canola (1 cup), 1927 calories 218 grams fat	Canola oil (½ cup) & unsweetened applesauce (½ cup), 987.50 calories, 109.12 grams fat	939.50 calories, 108.88 grams fat
Oil for frying, olive (5 tbsp), 595 calories, 67.5 grams fat	Onion (½ cup) with dried basil (1 tsp) in water, 35 calories, .14 grams fat	560 calories, 67.36 grams fat
Sour cream, for cooking (1 cup), 444 calories, 45.38 grams fat	Lemon juice (1 tbsp), plus evaporated milk (to equal 1 cup), 343 calories, 19.09 grams fat	101 calories, 26.29 grams fat
Spaghetti (1 cup), 220 calories, 1.3 grams fat	Bean sprouts (1 cup), 26 calories, .11 grams fat	194 calories, 1.19 grams fat
Spaghetti (1 cup), 220 calories, 1.3 grams fat	Spaghetti squash (1 cup), 42 calories, .40 grams fat	178 calories, .9 grams fat
Spaghetti sauce, marinara (1 cup), 224 calories, 6.91 grams fat	Canned tomatoes in tomato juice (1 cup), 41 calories, 0 grams fat	183 calories, 6.91 grams fat
Sugar, granulated, for baking (1 cup), 774 calories, 0 grams fat	Sugar, granulated (¾ cup), 580.5 calories, 0 grams fat	193.5 calories, 0 grams fat
Tuna, light, in oil (1 can drained), 339 calories, 14.04 grams fat	Tuna, light, in water (1 can drained), 191 calories, 1.35 grams fat	148 calories, 12.69 grams fat

Of course, making menu choices based on calories and fats isn't the only way to decide on dinner. You think in terms of the nutrients you are getting as well. More of each means better health and more satisfaction. Eating well is one of life's pleasures. Just strike the best balance you can between nutritional benefits and the undesirables: extra fats, calories, sodium, etc.,—and get on with it!

Here are some options that may help you achieve your goals and feel more satisfied with your diet and with your life.

Meats: Limit saturated fats to 10% of your total calories by choosing leaner cuts of meat, such as tenderloin, sirloin, chuck, or round.

Bread, cereal, rice, pasta, and flour: Choosing heartier whole grain versions over refined, "white" versions means more protein, fiber, and other nutrients, like selenium, potassium, and magnesium. They also make you feel full longer, and lower insulin, making you less likely to store fat. The Mayo Clinic says to choose items with at least 3 grams of dietary fiber per serving.

Breakfast cereal: Choose whole grain (see above) alternatives, such as bran flakes, shredded wheat, or old-fashioned oatmeal. (Check the labels for sodium levels before you buy.)

Chocolate: Got flavonoids? Choose dark chocolate over milk or other chocolate. It provides antioxidants, may lower blood pressure, and its flavonoids can improve mood and pleasure. Choose dark chocolate with a cacao content of 60% or more to reap the benefits. Enjoy a small piece a day.

Citrus: Eating a whole orange instead of drinking orange juice saves calories and carbs/sugar and provides more fiber.

Crackers: Pick crunchy, whole grain, heart healthy, low sodium varieties for added flavor and fiber and less fat.

Seasoning: If you use salt, try controlled pinchfuls of coarse kosher salt crystals (instead of using the salt shaker) as professional chefs do.

Fats: These should comprise about 15%–25% of your daily diet (and saturated fats 10%). Go for the smart stuff for your brain, heart, and belly—canola, olive, peanut, and sesame oils; nuts (pecans, walnuts, almonds, pistachios, etc.—but only a handful of each!), dark chocolate (see page 23), and avocados. Avoid high fat dairy products, fried foods, margarine, shortening, and lard.

Pasta: Robust whole wheat pasta can triple the fiber of regular pasta; it's made from flour that uses the entire grain seed. Pair it with bold sauces for more satisfying and nutritious meals. Or boost protein, energy, fiber, and flavor with super grain (actually a seed) quinoa ("keen-wah") instead of pasta and rice (even brown rice).

Salads: Add romaine and spinach to iceberg lettuce for more nutrients. Try new toppings: protein packed hard-boiled eggs or heart healthy pumpkin seeds, sunflower seeds, ground flax seed, walnuts, or almonds.

Side dishes: Cooking lentils instead of rice fills you up with more fiber and nutrients.

Yogurt: Greek yogurt delivers more protein, more creamy flavor, and much less sugar than fruit flavored counterparts.

YOUR RECIPES

In this section, you can write down your own recipes. Name each recipe, and fill in the story behind it. If it's an adaptation of something passed along from Grandma, record that fact for posterity.

Fill in the prep time, cooking time, number of servings, and ingredients. Write directions step by step. There's even a place for notes. The section is divided into seven categories:

For Starters
A place for appetizing appetizers and party delights

Salads and Dressings
Mainstays of your healthy diet

Favorite Soups
Soul satisfying concoctions

Meat and Poultry
Your beef, pork, and bird recipes corralled in one place!

Meatless and Fish
Creative meatless entrées, memorable fish dishes

On the Side
Veggies, pastas, and more

On the Sweeter Side
Treats and happy mealtime endings

Each category starts with bonus recipes (with estimated nutrients per serving) from chefs of several of North America's best restaurants, as well as sought-after personal chefs, and chefs who teach other chefs. It's as if you held a recipe exchange with some of the continent's top cooks! (And see page 228 for helpful Web sites and sites that allow you to enter your ingredients online for nutritional information at a few clicks of the mouse.)

FOR
STARTERS

RECIPE Grilled Smoked Salmon Flat Bread

SERVINGS 6   CALORIES 214   FAT 8.52 g   CARBS 25.28 g

FIBER 1.2 g   PROTEIN 14.89 g

SOURCE OF RECIPE Recipe courtesy of Chef Martin Laprise,

The Chef in Stead, Okanagan Valley, British Columbia

PREP TIME / COOK TIME 5 min. / 3-4 min., + 8 min. to assemble

INGREDIENTS

1 twelve-inch pizza crust, or naan bread

1 tablespoon extra virgin olive oil

⅔ pound smoked salmon per crust

¾ cup nonfat yogurt

Dill to taste

Lemon zest to taste

Salt and pepper to taste

Green onion or chives, chopped

INSTRUCTIONS

Grill the bread; then remove it from the heat and brush it with olive oil.

Spread the smoked salmon evenly on the bread.

In a cup or small bowl, mix the yogurt with dill, lemon zest, salt, and pepper.

Add the yogurt mixture to the salmon bread.

Top with green onions or chives.

Splash a touch more olive oil if you wish!

NOTES Nutritional estimates are per serving using pizza crust

RECIPE Tuna Tataki

SERVINGS 6 CALORIES 133 FAT 8.21 g CARBS 10.05 g

FIBER 3.6 g   PROTEIN 6.51 g

SOURCE OF RECIPE Recipe courtesy of Rob Feenie, Food Concept Architect, Cactus Club Restaurants, Alberta and British Columbia

PREP TIME / COOK TIME   20 min./1 min. or less

INGREDIENTS

Vinaigrette	Seared Tuna Tataki
2 teaspoons yuzu juice, or	4 ounces tuna loin
lime juice if not available	Salt and pepper to taste
1 tablespoon soy sauce	1 tablespoon olive oil
1 teaspoon garlic, minced	1 orange, in segments
1 tablespoon rice wine vinegar	1 avocado, diced
1 teaspoon lemon juice	1 papaya, diced
2 teaspoons olive oil	1 tablespoon pine nuts
Black pepper to taste	Cilantro for garnish

Green Papaya Slaw

2 tablespoons daikon radish, julienne

2 tablespoons carrots, julienne

2 tablespoons green papaya, julienne

1 teaspoon Thai basil

1 teaspoon mint

INSTRUCTIONS

In a small bowl, whisk the vinaigrette ingredients together.

Toss the slaw ingredients with the vinaigrette and mix until coated.

Pat the tuna dry with paper towels and season the fish with salt and pepper.

Heat a sauté pan with oil. Lightly sear the tuna for 10 seconds on each side.

Wrap the tuna tightly with plastic wrap and place it in the refrigerator. When fully chilled, slice the tuna into slices that are ¼-inch thick.

Place the dressed green papaya slaw on a plate. Garnish with orange, avocado, papaya, and pine nuts.

Fan tuna slices over the slaw and drizzle the remaining vinaigrette on top.

Garnish with cilantro.

NOTES

RECIPE

SERVINGS   CALORIES   FAT   CARBS

FIBER   PROTEIN

SOURCE OF RECIPE

PREP TIME / COOK TIME

INGREDIENTS

INSTRUCTIONS

NOTES

RECIPE

SERVINGS   CALORIES   FAT   CARBS

FIBER   PROTEIN

SOURCE OF RECIPE

PREP TIME / COOK TIME

INGREDIENTS

INSTRUCTIONS

NOTES

RECIPE

SERVINGS   CALORIES   FAT   CARBS

FIBER   PROTEIN

SOURCE OF RECIPE

PREP TIME / COOK TIME

INGREDIENTS

INSTRUCTIONS

NOTES

RECIPE

SERVINGS   CALORIES   FAT   CARBS

FIBER   PROTEIN

SOURCE OF RECIPE

PREP TIME / COOK TIME

INGREDIENTS

INSTRUCTIONS

NOTES

RECIPE

SERVINGS   CALORIES   FAT   CARBS

FIBER   PROTEIN

SOURCE OF RECIPE

PREP TIME / COOK TIME

INGREDIENTS

INSTRUCTIONS

NOTES

RECIPE

SERVINGS   CALORIES   FAT   CARBS

FIBER   PROTEIN

SOURCE OF RECIPE   .

PREP TIME / COOK TIME

INGREDIENTS

INSTRUCTIONS

NOTES

RECIPE

SERVINGS   CALORIES   FAT   CARBS

FIBER   PROTEIN

SOURCE OF RECIPE

PREP TIME / COOK TIME

INGREDIENTS

INSTRUCTIONS

NOTES

RECIPE

SERVINGS   CALORIES   FAT   CARBS

FIBER   PROTEIN

SOURCE OF RECIPE

PREP TIME / COOK TIME

INGREDIENTS

INSTRUCTIONS

NOTES

RECIPE

SERVINGS   CALORIES   FAT   CARBS

FIBER   PROTEIN

SOURCE OF RECIPE

PREP TIME / COOK TIME

INGREDIENTS

INSTRUCTIONS

NOTES

RECIPE

SERVINGS   CALORIES   FAT   CARBS

FIBER   PROTEIN

SOURCE OF RECIPE

PREP TIME / COOK TIME

INGREDIENTS

INSTRUCTIONS

NOTES

RECIPE

SERVINGS   CALORIES   FAT   CARBS

FIBER   PROTEIN

SOURCE OF RECIPE

PREP TIME / COOK TIME

INGREDIENTS

INSTRUCTIONS

NOTES

RECIPE

SERVINGS   CALORIES   FAT   CARBS

FIBER   PROTEIN

SOURCE OF RECIPE

PREP TIME / COOK TIME

INGREDIENTS

INSTRUCTIONS

NOTES

SALADS
AND DRESSINGS

RECIPE Truffled Lentil Salad with Arugula and Market Vegetables

SERVINGS 6 CALORIES 236 FAT 7.28 g CARBS 30.08 g

FIBER 6.7 g PROTEIN 13.92 g

SOURCE OF RECIPE Recipe courtesy of Chef Ryan Hutmacher, CEO, Centered Chef Food Studios, Chicago, Illinois

PREP TIME / COOK TIME 15-30 min./20 min.

INGREDIENTS

Lentil Salad

1½ cups French green lentils, picked over and rinsed

4 cups water

2 sprigs fresh thyme

1 bay leaf

Salt and pepper to taste

6 cups baby arugula

Truffled Vinaigrette

2 teaspoons Dijon mustard

2 teaspoons sherry vinegar

3 tablespoons orange juice

3 tablespoons truffle oil
(or extra virgin olive oil if truffle oil unavailable)

1 teaspoon chopped parsley

1½ teaspoons minced shallots

Salt and pepper to taste

Vegetables

(Choose just one or choose them all.)

3 red bell peppers, sliced

1 bunch French radishes, trimmed

1 bunch small golden beets, roasted, skinned, and thinly sliced

1 pound yellow wax beans, trimmed, blanched, and shocked

1 pound small new potatoes, scrubbed and boiled in salted water

INSTRUCTIONS

In a medium saucepan, combine the lentils, water, thyme sprigs, and bay leaf. Bring to a boil and season with salt.

Reduce the heat to medium low, and simmer uncovered until the lentils are tender, about 20 minutes.

Drain the lentils, discard the thyme and bay leaf, and allow the lentils to cool.

Make the vinaigrette: Place the mustard, vinegar, and orange juice in a small mixing bowl and stir to combine.

Slowly whisk in the oil in a steady stream.

Stir in the parsley and shallots and season to taste with salt and pepper.

Place the arugula in a large bowl and toss with just enough of the vinaigrette to lightly coat it.

Toss the rest of the vinaigrette with the lentils. Season to taste with salt and pepper.

Using a large platter, mound the lentils in the center. Arrange the arugula around the lentils, and place the vegetables on the sides.

NOTES Nutrition estimates are per serving for the Lentil Salad and Truffled Vinaigrette, and do not include side vegetables.

RECIPE

SERVINGS   CALORIES   FAT   CARBS

FIBER   PROTEIN

SOURCE OF RECIPE

PREP TIME / COOK TIME

INGREDIENTS

INSTRUCTIONS

NOTES

RECIPE

SERVINGS   CALORIES   FAT   CARBS

FIBER   PROTEIN

SOURCE OF RECIPE

PREP TIME / COOK TIME

INGREDIENTS

INSTRUCTIONS

NOTES

RECIPE

SERVINGS   CALORIES   FAT   CARBS

FIBER   PROTEIN

SOURCE OF RECIPE

PREP TIME / COOK TIME

INGREDIENTS

INSTRUCTIONS

NOTES

RECIPE

SERVINGS   CALORIES   FAT   CARBS

FIBER   PROTEIN

SOURCE OF RECIPE

PREP TIME / COOK TIME

INGREDIENTS

INSTRUCTIONS

NOTES

RECIPE

SERVINGS   CALORIES   FAT   CARBS

FIBER   PROTEIN

SOURCE OF RECIPE

PREP TIME / COOK TIME

INGREDIENTS

INSTRUCTIONS

NOTES

RECIPE

SERVINGS   CALORIES   FAT   CARBS

FIBER   PROTEIN

SOURCE OF RECIPE

PREP TIME / COOK TIME

INGREDIENTS

INSTRUCTIONS

NOTES

RECIPE

SERVINGS   CALORIES   FAT   CARBS

FIBER   PROTEIN

SOURCE OF RECIPE

PREP TIME / COOK TIME

INGREDIENTS

INSTRUCTIONS

NOTES

RECIPE

SERVINGS   CALORIES   FAT   CARBS

FIBER   PROTEIN

SOURCE OF RECIPE

PREP TIME / COOK TIME

INGREDIENTS

INSTRUCTIONS

NOTES

RECIPE

SERVINGS   CALORIES   FAT   CARBS

FIBER   PROTEIN

SOURCE OF RECIPE

PREP TIME / COOK TIME

INGREDIENTS

INSTRUCTIONS

NOTES

RECIPE

SERVINGS   CALORIES   FAT   CARBS

FIBER   PROTEIN

SOURCE OF RECIPE

PREP TIME / COOK TIME

INGREDIENTS

_____

_____

_____

_____

_____

_____

_____

_____

_____

_____

_____

_____

_____

_____

_____

_____

_____

_____

_____

_____

_____

_____

INSTRUCTIONS

NOTES

RECIPE

SERVINGS   CALORIES   FAT   CARBS

FIBER   PROTEIN

SOURCE OF RECIPE

PREP TIME / COOK TIME

INGREDIENTS

INSTRUCTIONS

NOTES

RECIPE

SERVINGS   CALORIES   FAT   CARBS

FIBER   PROTEIN

SOURCE OF RECIPE

PREP TIME / COOK TIME

INGREDIENTS

INSTRUCTIONS

_____

_____

_____

_____

_____

_____

_____

_____

_____

_____

_____

_____

_____

_____

_____

_____

_____

_____

_____

_____

_____

_____

NOTES

_____

_____

_____

FAVORITE
SOUPS

RECIPE Chilled Pea Soup with Smoked Chicken and Mint Yogurt

SERVINGS 12 CALORIES 203 FAT 2.6 g   CARBS 31.46 g

FIBER 9 g   PROTEIN 14.75 g

SOURCE OF RECIPE Recipe courtesy of Andre Molle, Executive Chef,
Le Chateau Restaurant, South Salem, New York

PREP TIME / COOK TIME 15-20 min./30 min., + 4 hrs. to chill

INGREDIENTS

5 pounds frozen peas

1 teaspoon canola oil

2 leeks, medium, washed and sliced

2 onions, medium, minced

2 cloves garlic, chopped

6 cups water

6 cups low sodium chicken stock

Salt and pepper to taste

Dash of Tabasco

3 tablespoons low fat yogurt

12 leaves fresh mint, chopped

6 ounces smoked chicken breast, diced (optional)

1 plum tomato, peeled and diced

12 sprigs chervil

INSTRUCTIONS

In a large pot, bring 2 gallons of water to a rolling boil, then add the peas and return to a rapid boil.

Drain the water and transfer the peas to a large bowl of iced water. Drain peas again and set them aside.

In a pot, heat the canola oil. Add leeks and onions. Sweat for 8 to 10 minutes. Add the garlic, water, and chicken stock. Simmer for 30 minutes. Add the peas and simmer for 5 minutes. Season with salt and pepper.

Purée the soup in a blender, working in small batches. Strain through a fine sieve to remove solids. Chill the soup over ice in a bowl, then refrigerate for 4 hours.

Taste and adjust the seasonings as needed. Add a dash of Tabasco. Mix the yogurt and mint.

Divide the chicken into 12 chilled bowls. Add the soup. Garnish with the yogurt/mint mixture. Place diced tomato and chervil on top.

NOTES Requires blender, fine sieve. Nutrition estimates are per serving, including optional chicken.

RECIPE Peanut Soup

SERVINGS 10   CALORIES 176   FAT 10.33 g   CARBS 17.94 g

FIBER 2.7 g   PROTEIN 6.23 g

SOURCE OF RECIPE Recipe courtesy of Gord Harris, Executive Chef,
Prairie Ink Restaurant and Bakery, Winnipeg and Saskatoon

PREP TIME / COOK TIME   20-25 min. / 45 min.

INGREDIENTS

⅜ cup carrots, diced

⅜ cup celery, diced

⅜ cup white onion, diced

1½ teaspoons olive oil

1½ cups sweet potatoes, peeled and chopped

Water, as needed to cover vegetables

1 cup reduced fat peanut butter, smooth

7 ounces whole tomatoes, canned

1½ teaspoons kosher salt (suggested)

¼ teaspoon Cayenne pepper (suggested)

INSTRUCTIONS

In a large pot over medium-high heat, sauté the carrots, celery, and onions in the olive oil for 3 to 4 minutes.

Add the sweet potatoes and cover the vegetables with water.

Bring to a boil and simmer until the potatoes are cooked.

Add the remaining ingredients and purée with a mixer or food processor until the mixture is smooth.

Adjust seasonings to taste.

NOTES Requires mixer or food processor

RECIPE

SERVINGS   CALORIES   FAT   CARBS

FIBER   PROTEIN

SOURCE OF RECIPE

PREP TIME / COOK TIME

INGREDIENTS

_____

_____

_____

_____

_____

_____

_____

_____

_____

_____

_____

_____

_____

_____

_____

_____

_____

_____

_____

_____

_____

INSTRUCTIONS

NOTES

RECIPE

SERVINGS   CALORIES   FAT   CARBS

FIBER   PROTEIN

SOURCE OF RECIPE

PREP TIME / COOK TIME

INGREDIENTS

INSTRUCTIONS

NOTES

RECIPE

SERVINGS   CALORIES   FAT   CARBS

FIBER   PROTEIN

SOURCE OF RECIPE

PREP TIME / COOK TIME

INGREDIENTS

INSTRUCTIONS

NOTES

RECIPE

SERVINGS   CALORIES   FAT   CARBS

FIBER   PROTEIN

SOURCE OF RECIPE

PREP TIME / COOK TIME

INGREDIENTS

INSTRUCTIONS

NOTES

RECIPE

SERVINGS   CALORIES   FAT   CARBS

FIBER   PROTEIN

SOURCE OF RECIPE

PREP TIME / COOK TIME

INGREDIENTS

INSTRUCTIONS

_____
_____
_____
_____
_____
_____
_____
_____
_____
_____
_____
_____
_____
_____
_____
_____
_____
_____
_____
_____
_____
_____

NOTES
_____
_____
_____

RECIPE

SERVINGS   CALORIES   FAT   CARBS

FIBER   PROTEIN

SOURCE OF RECIPE

PREP TIME / COOK TIME

INGREDIENTS

INSTRUCTIONS

_____

_____

_____

_____

_____

_____

_____

_____

_____

_____

_____

_____

_____

_____

_____

_____

_____

_____

_____

_____

_____

_____

NOTES

_____

_____

_____

RECIPE

SERVINGS   CALORIES   FAT   CARBS

FIBER   PROTEIN

SOURCE OF RECIPE

PREP TIME / COOK TIME

INGREDIENTS

INSTRUCTIONS

NOTES

RECIPE

SERVINGS   CALORIES   FAT   CARBS

FIBER   PROTEIN

SOURCE OF RECIPE

PREP TIME / COOK TIME

INGREDIENTS

INSTRUCTIONS

NOTES

RECITE

SERVINGS   CALORIES   FAT   CARBS

FIBER   PROTEIN

SOURCE OF RECIPE

PREP TIME / COOK TIME

INGREDIENTS

INSTRUCTIONS

NOTES

RECILE

SERVINGS   CALORIES   FAT   CARBS

FIBER   PROTEIN

SOURCE OF RECIPE

PREP TIME / COOK TIME

INGREDIENTS

INSTRUCTIONS

NOTES

RECICE

SERVINGS   CALORIES   FAT   CARBS

FIBER   PROTEIN

SOURCE OF RECIPE

PREP TIME / COOK TIME

INGREDIENTS

INSTRUCTIONS

NOTES

RECIPE

SERVINGS   CALORIES   FAT   CARBS

FIBER   PROTEIN

SOURCE OF RECIPE

PREP TIME / COOK TIME

INGREDIENTS

INSTRUCTIONS

NOTES

MEAT AND POULTRY

RECIPE	PAGE
Summer's Brick Chicken	116

RECIPE Summer's Brick Chicken

SERVINGS 6   CALORIES 400   FAT 15.19 g   CARBS 1.27 g

FIBER .08 g   PROTEIN 61.59 g

SOURCE OF RECIPE Recipe courtesy of Cathal Armstrong,
Chef-Owner, Restaurant Eve, Alexandria, Virginia

PREP TIME / COOK TIME   15 min./25-35 min.

INGREDIENTS

4 pounds grassfed chicken

5 cloves garlic

2 tablespoons fresh lemon juice

2 tablespoons fresh rosemary, chopped

¼ teaspoon dried red pepper, crushed

Coarse kosher salt

3 tablespoons olive oil

Rosemary sprigs and parsley leaves for garnish

INSTRUCTIONS

If using a whole chicken, butterfly it (there are videos on YouTube that show how). Or use bone-in breasts or quartered chicken if you don't want or have time to butterfly.

Make a rub: Smash the cloves of garlic with the side of your knife and chop fine. Mix in a small bowl with lemon juice, rosemary, a good dose of red pepper flakes, and kosher salt. Drizzle in olive oil. Rub mixture all over the bird and under the skin. Reserve some to pour over chicken when transferring to platter.

Allow marinade to drip from chicken, then place bird skin side down on grill on medium-low heat. Place foil-wrapped brick on top of chicken and grill for about 7 minutes until golden brown.

Remove the brick and turn chicken over.

Place the brick atop bird again and grill until golden and meat is no longer pink.

Remove brick and transfer chicken to platter.

Drizzle bird with remaining marinade.

Garnish with rosemary and parsley.

NOTES Requires grill and clean, foil-wrapped bricks. This Tuscan-inspired dish flattens the chicken, exposing maximum surface area to the heat of your grill, resulting in a crackling, crisp exterior.

RECIPE

SERVINGS   CALORIES   FAT   CARBS

FIBER   PROTEIN

SOURCE OF RECIPE

PREP TIME / COOK TIME

INGREDIENTS

INSTRUCTIONS

NOTES

RECIPE

SERVINGS   CALORIES   FAT   CARBS

FIBER   PROTEIN

SOURCE OF RECIPE

PREP TIME / COOK TIME

INGREDIENTS

INSTRUCTIONS

NOTES

RECIPE

SERVINGS   CALORIES   FAT   CARBS

FIBER   PROTEIN

SOURCE OF RECIPE

PREP TIME / COOK TIME

INGREDIENTS

_____

_____

_____

_____

_____

_____

_____

_____

_____

_____

_____

_____

_____

_____

_____

_____

_____

_____

_____

_____

_____

_____

INSTRUCTIONS

NOTES

RECIPE

SERVINGS   CALORIES   FAT   CARBS

FIBER   PROTEIN

SOURCE OF RECIPE

PREP TIME / COOK TIME

INGREDIENTS

INSTRUCTIONS

NOTES

RECIPE

SERVINGS   CALORIES   FAT   CARBS

FIBER   PROTEIN

SOURCE OF RECIPE

PREP TIME / COOK TIME

INGREDIENTS

INSTRUCTIONS

NOTES

RECITE

SERVINGS   CALORIES   FAT   CARBS

FIBER   PROTEIN

SOURCE OF RECIPE

PREP TIME / COOK TIME

INGREDIENTS

INSTRUCTIONS

NOTES

RECIPE

SERVINGS   CALORIES   FAT   CARBS

FIBER   PROTEIN

SOURCE OF RECIPE

PREP TIME / COOK TIME

INGREDIENTS

INSTRUCTIONS

NOTES

RECIPE

SERVINGS   CALORIES   FAT   CARBS

FIBER   PROTEIN

SOURCE OF RECIPE

PREP TIME / COOK TIME

INGREDIENTS

INSTRUCTIONS

NOTES

RECIPE

SERVINGS   CALORIES   FAT   CARBS

FIBER   PROTEIN

SOURCE OF RECIPE

PREP TIME / COOK TIME

INGREDIENTS

INSTRUCTIONS

NOTES

RECIPE

SERVINGS   CALORIES   FAT   CARBS

FIBER   PROTEIN

SOURCE OF RECIPE

PREP TIME / COOK TIME

INGREDIENTS

INSTRUCTIONS

NOTES

RECIPE

SERVINGS   CALORIES   FAT   CARBS

FIBER   PROTEIN

SOURCE OF RECIPE

PREP TIME / COOK TIME

INGREDIENTS

INSTRUCTIONS

NOTES

RECIPE

SERVINGS   CALORIES   FAT   CARBS

FIBER   PROTEIN

SOURCE OF RECIPE

PREP TIME / COOK TIME

INGREDIENTS

INSTRUCTIONS

NOTES

MEATLESS
AND FISH

RECIPE Baked Halibut with Lemon Basil Vinaigrette

SERVINGS 4 CALORIES 320 FAT 18 g CARBS 3.08 g

FIBER .70 g PROTEIN 35.96 g

SOURCE OF RECIPE Recipe courtesy of Karen Barnaby, Executive Chef, The Fish House in Stanley Park, Vancouver, British Columbia

PREP TIME / COOK TIME 15 min. / 10–12 min.

INGREDIENTS

4 six-ounce fresh halibut fillets*

Salt and pepper to taste

2 tablespoons fresh lemon juice

1 teaspoon lemon zest, grated

2 cloves garlic, cut in half

4 tablespoons olive oil

3 tablespoons fresh basil leaves, sliced thin

1 cup tomatoes, diced fine

INSTRUCTIONS

Preheat the oven to 350°F.

Season the halibut fillets with salt and pepper.

Lightly oil a baking dish and place the halibut in the dish, without overlapping the pieces. Bake for 10 to 12 minutes, until the fish is opaque all the way through.

While the fish is baking, make the vinaigrette. Combine the lemon juice and lemon zest in a small bowl. Add salt and pepper to taste. Spear garlic on the tines of a fork and use it to beat the lemon juice mixture.

Beat in the olive oil, and then stir in the basil and tomatoes. Discard the garlic.

Place the halibut on heated plates, spoon the vinaigrette on top, and serve.

NOTES Requires food processor, food mill. *You can use any fish with this vinaigrette, and it also goes well with prawns or scallops.

RECITE

SERVINGS   CALORIES   FAT   CARBS

FIBER   PROTEIN

SOURCE OF RECIPE

PREP TIME / COOK TIME

INGREDIENTS

INSTRUCTIONS

NOTES

RECIPE

SERVINGS   CALORIES   FAT   CARBS

FIBER   PROTEIN

SOURCE OF RECIPE

PREP TIME / COOK TIME

INGREDIENTS

INSTRUCTIONS

NOTES

RECIPE

SERVINGS   CALORIES   FAT   CARBS

FIBER   PROTEIN

SOURCE OF RECIPE

PREP TIME / COOK TIME

INGREDIENTS

INSTRUCTIONS

NOTES

RECIPE

SERVINGS   CALORIES   FAT   CARBS

FIBER   PROTEIN

SOURCE OF RECIPE

PREP TIME / COOK TIME

INGREDIENTS

INSTRUCTIONS

NOTES

RECIPE

SERVINGS   CALORIES   FAT   CARBS

FIBER   PROTEIN

SOURCE OF RECIPE

PREP TIME / COOK TIME

INGREDIENTS

INSTRUCTIONS

NOTES

RECIPE

SERVINGS   CALORIES   FAT   CARBS

FIBER   PROTEIN

SOURCE OF RECIPE

PREP TIME / COOK TIME

INGREDIENTS

INSTRUCTIONS

NOTES

RECIPE

SERVINGS　　CALORIES　　FAT　　CARBS

FIBER　　　　PROTEIN

SOURCE OF RECIPE

PREP TIME / COOK TIME

INGREDIENTS

INSTRUCTIONS

NOTES

RECIPE

SERVINGS　　CALORIES　　FAT　　　　CARBS

FIBER　　　　　PROTEIN

SOURCE OF RECIPE

PREP TIME / COOK TIME

INGREDIENTS

INSTRUCTIONS

NOTES

RECIPE

SERVINGS   CALORIES   FAT   CARBS

FIBER   PROTEIN

SOURCE OF RECIPE

PREP TIME / COOK TIME

INGREDIENTS

INSTRUCTIONS

NOTES

RECITE

SERVINGS   CALORIES   FAT   CARBS

FIBER   PROTEIN

SOURCE OF RECIPE

PREP TIME / COOK TIME

INGREDIENTS

INSTRUCTIONS

NOTES

RECIPE

SERVINGS   CALORIES   FAT   CARBS

FIBER   PROTEIN

SOURCE OF RECIPE

PREP TIME / COOK TIME

INGREDIENTS

INSTRUCTIONS

NOTES

ON THE
SIDE

RECIPE Farm Fresh Goat Cheese and Poblano Creamed Corn

SERVINGS 6 to 8 CALORIES 252   FAT 10.26 g   CARBS 35.24 g

FIBER 3.9 g   PROTEIN 9.94 g

SOURCE OF RECIPE Recipe courtesy of Laura Pensiero, Chef, Author,

and Registered Dietician*

PREP TIME / COOK TIME 15–20 min./20 min.

INGREDIENTS

6 ears fresh corn, or about 4 to 5 cups kernels

2 tablespoons olive oil

2 shallots, peeled and minced

2 poblano peppers, seeded and diced

2 garlic cloves, minced

2 tablespoons flat-leaf parsley, chopped

Salt and freshly ground pepper

¼ cup dry white wine (optional)

2 teaspoons sugar (optional; use if the corn is not sweet enough)

1 tablespoon flour, blended with 2 tablespoons water

1 ⅓ cups 1% milk

1 tablespoon cilantro, chopped

3 ounces crumbled goat cheese (or queso blanco, feta, or
    shredded cheddar)

¼ cup reduced-fat Parmesan cheese, grated (optional)

INSTRUCTIONS

Cut the kernels from the corncobs, then scrape the cobs with a sharp knife to get all the milky corn liquid and pulp; reserve the kernels separately from the liquid and pulp.

Heat the olive oil in a large skillet over medium heat. Add the shallots, poblanos, and garlic. Cook, stirring, until vegetables soften, 3 or 4 minutes.

Increase heat to medium high, stir in the kernels, half of the parsley, and season with salt and pepper. Cook, tossing or stirring often, until the kernels are cooked and lightly brown, about 4 minutes.

Add the reserved pulp, milky corn liquid, and the white wine and sugar (if you are using these optional ingredients). Cook until liquid has almost completely evaporated.

Stir in the flour-water mixture. Whisk in the 1% milk. Bring the mixture to a simmer and cook, stirring, until thickened, about 3 minutes.

Add salt and pepper to taste. Stir in remaining parsley and the cilantro. Remove from heat and stir in the goat cheese.

Serve immediately, or transfer to oven-safe crocks or ramekins, sprinkle the tops with Parmesan (optional), and broil under high heat until the tops are bubbly and brown.

NOTES Nutrition estimates are per serving without optional ingredients. *Laura is also owner of Gigi Hudson Valley, New York State (Trattoria, Market, Catering), and partner at Just Salad, New York and Hong Kong.

RECIPE Long Green Beans and New Potatoes in Mustard Seed Curry

SERVINGS 6   CALORIES 247   FAT 19.89 g   CARBS 17.91 g

FIBER 4.6 g   PROTEIN 3.75 g

SOURCE OF RECIPE From the cookbook "Vij's: Elegant & Inspired

Indian Cuisine"*

PREP TIME / COOK TIME 20-30 min. / 30-40 min.

INGREDIENTS

9 ounces new potatoes

½ cup canola oil

1½ tablespoons cumin seeds

3 cups puréed tomatoes (about 6 large)

1 tablespoon black mustard seeds, ground

1 tablespoon salt

1 tablespoon cayenne pepper, crushed

1 teaspoon turmeric

4⅓ cups water

9 ounces green beans, strings removed, cut in half lengthwise

INSTRUCTIONS

Soak new potatoes in water for 10 minutes to loosen any dirt. Drain and thoroughly wash the potatoes, then cut each one in 4 to 6 slices. Set aside.

In a medium pot, heat oil on high for 1 minute. Sprinkle in the cumin seeds, stir, and allow seeds to sizzle for about 30 seconds. Reduce the heat to medium and add tomatoes, mustard seeds, salt, cayenne, and turmeric. Stir well and cook this masala for 5 to 8 minutes, or until oil glistens on top.

Stir in the water and bring to boil on medium-high heat for 8 to 10 minutes, stirring occasionally. If the curry still seems very runny and watery, boil for another 5 minutes. The spices and the water should be very well mixed together at the end of boiling. Turn down the heat to medium-low. Add the potatoes and cook at a medium boil, covered, for 5 to 8 minutes.

Add green beans, stir well, and cook, uncovered, for 5 minutes. Serve piping hot in individual bowls.

NOTES *© 2006, by Meeru Dhalwala & Vikram Vij, published by Douglas & McIntyre: an imprint of D&M Publishers Inc. Reprinted with permission of the publisher.

RECIPE

SERVINGS   CALORIES   FAT   CARBS

FIBER   PROTEIN

SOURCE OF RECIPE

PREP TIME / COOK TIME

INGREDIENTS

INSTRUCTIONS

NOTES

RECIPE

SERVINGS   CALORIES   FAT   CARBS

FIBER   PROTEIN

SOURCE OF RECIPE

PREP TIME / COOK TIME

INGREDIENTS

INSTRUCTIONS

NOTES

RECIPE

SERVINGS   CALORIES   FAT   CARBS

FIBER   PROTEIN

SOURCE OF RECIPE

PREP TIME / COOK TIME

INGREDIENTS

INSTRUCTIONS

NOTES

RECIPE

SERVINGS   CALORIES   FAT   CARBS

FIBER   PROTEIN

SOURCE OF RECIPE

PREP TIME / COOK TIME

INGREDIENTS

INSTRUCTIONS

NOTES

RECIPE

SERVINGS   CALORIES   FAT   CARBS

FIBER   PROTEIN

SOURCE OF RECIPE

PREP TIME / COOK TIME

INGREDIENTS

INSTRUCTIONS

NOTES

RECIPE

SERVINGS   CALORIES   FAT   CARBS

FIBER   PROTEIN

SOURCE OF RECIPE

PREP TIME / COOK TIME

INGREDIENTS

INSTRUCTIONS

NOTES

RECIPE

SERVINGS   CALORIES   FAT   CARBS

FIBER   PROTEIN

SOURCE OF RECIPE

PREP TIME / COOK TIME

INGREDIENTS

INSTRUCTIONS

NOTES

RECIPE

SERVINGS   CALORIES   FAT   CARBS

FIBER   PROTEIN

SOURCE OF RECIPE

PREP TIME / COOK TIME

INGREDIENTS

INSTRUCTIONS

NOTES

RECICE

SERVINGS   CALORIES   FAT   CARBS

FIBER   PROTEIN

SOURCE OF RECIPE

PREP TIME / COOK TIME

INGREDIENTS

INSTRUCTIONS

NOTES

RECITE

SERVINGS   CALORIES   FAT   CARBS

FIBER   PROTEIN

SOURCE OF RECIPE

PREP TIME / COOK TIME

INGREDIENTS

INSTRUCTIONS

NOTES

ON THE
SWEETER SIDE

RECIPE Mixed Berry Granita with Mint

SERVINGS 16   CALORIES 74   FAT .13 g   CARBS 18.66 g

FIBER .80 g   PROTEIN .55 g

SOURCE OF RECIPE Recipe courtesy of Chef Ryan Hutmacher, CEO,
Centered Chef Food Studios, Chicago, Illinois

PREP TIME / COOK TIME 15 min. / 10 min.

INGREDIENTS

4 cups unsweetened grape juice

½ cup sugar

2 tablespoons fresh mint leaves

1 cup raspberries

1 cup blueberries

½ cup lemon juice

1 teaspoon orange zest

Sparkling water or Champagne (optional)

INSTRUCTIONS

Bring the grape juice and sugar to a boil and cook until the sugar dissolves. Remove the mixture from the heat.

In a food processor, add the mint, berries, and enough of the hot grape juice solution to keep the mixture moving. Pulse until smooth.

Filter the berry purée over a wide baking dish using a mesh strainer. (Ensure that the pan is flat.)

Add the remaining hot grape juice solution through the strainer, using the back of a ladle to help push liquid through.

Stir in the lemon juice and orange zest.

Let mixture cool down to room temperature, and then place in the freezer.

For quicker freezing, stir with a fork every hour, or use a larger pan with more surface area. Keep the mix in the freezer until the liquid is completely frozen.

For serving, use a fork to scrape the granita loose. Serve mounded in a martini glass with sparkling water or Champagne, if desired.

NOTES Requires food processor and mesh strainer. Nutrition estimates per serving: Champagne not included. Try swapping in 1/4 cup of Splenda Sugar Blend for the 1/2 cup of sugar to save more calories.

RECIPE

SERVINGS   CALORIES   FAT   CARBS

FIBER   PROTEIN

SOURCE OF RECIPE

PREP TIME / COOK TIME

INGREDIENTS

INSTRUCTIONS

NOTES

RECIPE

SERVINGS   CALORIES   FAT   CARBS

FIBER   PROTEIN

SOURCE OF RECIPE

PREP TIME / COOK TIME

INGREDIENTS

INSTRUCTIONS

NOTES

RECIPE

SERVINGS   CALORIES   FAT   CARBS

FIBER   PROTEIN

SOURCE OF RECIPE

PREP TIME / COOK TIME

INGREDIENTS

INSTRUCTIONS

NOTES

RECIPE

SERVINGS   CALORIES   FAT   CARBS

FIBER   PROTEIN

SOURCE OF RECIPE

PREP TIME / COOK TIME

INGREDIENTS

INSTRUCTIONS

NOTES

RECIPE

SERVINGS   CALORIES   FAT   CARBS

FIBER   PROTEIN

SOURCE OF RECIPE

PREP TIME / COOK TIME

INGREDIENTS

INSTRUCTIONS

NOTES

RECICPE

SERVINGS   CALORIES   FAT   CARBS

FIBER   PROTEIN

SOURCE OF RECIPE

PREP TIME / COOK TIME

INGREDIENTS

INSTRUCTIONS

NOTES

RECIPE

SERVINGS   CALORIES   FAT   CARBS

FIBER   PROTEIN

SOURCE OF RECIPE

PREP TIME / COOK TIME

INGREDIENTS

INSTRUCTIONS

NOTES

RECIPE

SERVINGS   CALORIES   FAT   CARBS

FIBER   PROTEIN

SOURCE OF RECIPE

PREP TIME / COOK TIME

INGREDIENTS

INSTRUCTIONS

NOTES

RECIPE

SERVINGS   CALORIES   FAT   CARBS

FIBER   PROTEIN

SOURCE OF RECIPE

PREP TIME / COOK TIME

INGREDIENTS

INSTRUCTIONS

NOTES

RECIPE

SERVINGS   CALORIES   FAT   CARBS

FIBER   PROTEIN

SOURCE OF RECIPE

PREP TIME / COOK TIME

INGREDIENTS

INSTRUCTIONS

NOTES

RECIPE

SERVINGS   CALORIES   FAT   CARBS

FIBER   PROTEIN

SOURCE OF RECIPE

PREP TIME / COOK TIME

INGREDIENTS

INSTRUCTIONS

NOTES

RECIPE

SERVINGS   CALORIES   FAT   CARBS

FIBER   PROTEIN

SOURCE OF RECIPE

PREP TIME / COOK TIME

INGREDIENTS

INSTRUCTIONS

NOTES

RESOURCES

When you want to find the nutritional values for your recipes, visit the USDA Nutrient Database at **http://www.nal.usda.gov/fnic/foodcomp/search/**. Follow the prompts, which will give you options for serving sizes and offer ways to adjust the measures and amounts. You might also like exploring the following sites:

> **www.caloriecountercharts.com**
> **www.thedailyplate.com***
> **www.fatsecret.com***
> **www.foodsubs.com**
> **www.hungry-girl.com**
> **www.weightwatchers.com**

*These sites have recipe builders that allow you to "plug in" ingredients and obtain nutrition information.

MEASURE TO MEASURE

Also see **http://www.ars.usda.gov/Aboutus/docs.htm?docid=9617**

Measure Equivalents

Unit	Equals	Also equals
1 tbsp	½ fl. oz	3 tsp
⅛ cup	1 fl. oz	2 tbsp
¼ cup	2 fl. oz	4 tbsp
⅓ cup	2¾ fl. oz	¼ cup + 4 tsp or 5 tbsp + 1 tsp
½ cup	4 fl. oz	8 tbsp
1 cup	8 fl. oz	½ pint or 48 tsp or 16 tbsp
1 pint	16 fl. oz	2 cups
1 quart	32 fl. oz	2 pints
1 liter	34 fl. oz	1 quart plus ¼ cup
1 gallon	128 fl. oz	4 quarts

MASTERING METRIC

Most of the world's cooks use the metric system when weighing food in the kitchen. This chart can help you convert recipes from the metric system to the U.S. system of units or vice versa.

Metric Conversion Factors

Multiply	By	To Get
fluid ounces	29.57	grams
ounces (dry)	28.35	grams
grams	0.0353	ounces
grams	0.0022	pounds
kilograms	2.21	pounds
pounds	453.6	grams
pounds	0.4536	kilograms
quarts	0.946	liters
liters	1.0567	quarts
gallons	3.785	liters

MY RECIPE INDEX

RECITE NAME   JOURNAL PAGE

MEAT AND POULTRY

MEATLESS AND FISH

ON THE SIDE

_____

_____

_____

_____

_____

_____

_____

_____

_____

_____

ON THE SWEETER SIDE

_____

_____

_____

_____

_____

_____

_____

_____

_____

_____